CLONMACNOISE

CLONMACNOISE

OPW

Oifig na nOibreacha Poiblí
The Office of Public Works

Introduction

I T IS JUST AN ACCIDENT OF HISTORY THAT CLONMACNOISE TODAY IS NOT AN important cathedral town and major crossing point of the Shannon. Such was its great importance between c700 and 1200 AD, that its population would probably have confidently expected this major centre of piety, learning, trade and craftsmanship to have continued to grow in importance up to the last day. How lucky we are that it declined, and that instead of a busy modern town with its traffic and noise strangling the much-altered remnants of an early monastery, we find the extensive remains of buildings and crosses surviving in the peace and quiet of their outstanding rural setting on the banks of the Shannon.

Ironically, in its present-day unspoilt tranquillity, it probably more closely resembles the site which St Ciarán chose for his monastery in the mid-sixth century than the clamorous, busy, congested settlement it grew into some centuries later. Of all the monastic centres of this period in Ireland, Clonmacnoise was second only in importance to Armagh, and probably surpassed Armagh in its artistic and literary achievements.

Close-up aerial view of the main group of monuments, including the Cathedral and Round Tower, with Temples Connor, Ciarán, Melaghlin, Hurpan and Dowling running clockwise from the back.

frontispiece – Aerial view of Clonmacnoise from the south-west showing the main site, with the river Shannon meandering around the adjacent area of natural water meadows called 'callows', and the raised bogland across the river in the background

The Setting

CLONMACNOISE IS SITUATED CLOSE TO THE CENTRE OF THE COUNTRY ON A gravel ridge overlooking the river Shannon, the longest river in Ireland. Nowadays, a detour off the main road is necessary to get there, but formerly its location on two major routeways – the river itself running north/south, and a band of glacial eskers carrying the main east/west route across the country – meant that it was situated literally at the main crossroads of Ireland.

The other major component of the landscape is raised bog, which largely confined overland traffic to the dry sandy eskers. Great variation in river levels between winter and summer alters the scene dramatically through the seasons. This is particularly true of the low-lying meadows to the north-east of the site, known as the callows, which are submerged by the rising waters of the river each winter.

The variety of land types in the immediate area with their flora and fauna makes the place important ecologically as well as historically. There are the eskers, the callows, the raised bogs, an area of bare limestone rock at Clorhane on the way to Shannonbridge, and the remnants of a lake at Finlough. Mongan Bog, to the north of the Athlone Road, is a protected area owned by An Taisce, Ireland's National Trust.

An early nineteenth-century engraving of
Clonmacnoise, viewed from across the
Shannon, based on an original drawing by
George Petrie

The Cross of the Scriptures with the river
and castle in the background, as depicted by
Henry O'Neill (1857)

Early History

THE MONASTERY WAS FOUNDED BY ST CIARÁN IN THE MIDDLE OF THE SIXTH century. Different sets of annals give dates varying between 543 and 549 as the date of his death, but virtually all are agreed that he founded the monastery either in the same year as his death or in the previous year. The 'lives' of the saint, written many centuries later but presumably incorporating early tradition, state that he lived for only seven months or a year after the foundation of Clonmacnoise. They also record that he was not of noble birth like many other Irish saints, but was the son of a craftsman and had founded a community on Hare Island in Lough Ree, further north on the Shannon, before settling at Clonmacnoise. The name Cluain Mhic Nóis in Irish means the meadow of the sons of Nós and appears to predate the founding of the monastery. Despite Ciarán's death within a year of its foundation, the monastery seems to have grown rapidly in importance and fame. Its location, just within the territory of Mide (Meath) on its border with Connacht, meant that it could have close associations with both provinces.

It is recounted in Adamnán's *Life of Columba*, which was written c690, that St Columba (Columcille) visited Clonmacnoise during the abbacy of Alither (c585-599):

> When they heard of his approach, all those that were in the fields near the monastery came from every side, and joined those that were within it, and with the utmost eagerness accompanying their abbot Alither they passed outside the boundary-wall of the monastery, and with one accord went to meet Saint Columba, as if he had been an angel of the Lord.

It appears that already in the seventh century, monasteries such as Clonmacnoise were losing sight of some of their founders' ideals and were becoming partly secularised and worldly. Large monasteries had dependent monasteries and churches attached to them, known collectively as a paruchia, and disputes arose between important monasteries over such matters. Tírechán, writing about St Patrick around 700 AD, complained that the community of Clonmacnoise forcibly held many churches founded by St Patrick. Matters must have come to a very serious pass between Clonmacnoise and the Columban foundation of Durrow in 764, for in that year a pitched battle was fought between the two communities in which the latter were beaten with a loss of 200 men. Despite the decline in religious standards, some members of the community would have continued to lead exemplary lives. It was as a reaction against abuses that a reform movement calling themselves the Céli Dé developed in the eighth century, and while Clonmacnoise never became a Céli Dé monastery as such, smaller groups and anchorites in the Céli Dé tradition existed within the monastery.

The Irish annals record the deaths of many of the abbots here, and it is possible to compile an almost complete succession list of abbots from Ciarán up to the twelfth century. They also record that the monastery was burned on three occasions in the eighth century, but do not indicate whether these burnings were malicious or accidental. Frequent burnings of parts of the settlement continue into the ninth century, accompanied by references to more clearly deliberate destruction. By this time, the Vikings had started to plunder monasteries in Ireland, but the first recorded raid was by an Irish king, Feidlimid Mac Crimthainn of Cashel, in 833, when he killed many people there and 'burned their church-lands to the very door of their church'. The first recorded Viking raid was the plundering in 842 by 'heathens from Linn Duchaill'. This was followed in 845 with a raid by Vikings encamped on Lough Ree, who burned Clonmacnoise with its oratories.

Two pages from *Lebor na hUidhre* (*The Book of the Dun Cow*) written at Clonmacnoise c1100 AD, and now in the Royal Irish Academy

The Golden Age
of the Monastery

ABOUT THIRTY SUBSEQUENT PLUNDERINGS AND BURNINGS, THE VAST majority perpetrated by the Irish themselves, are recorded up to the middle of the twelfth century. Yet the vitality, power and importance of the settlement does not seem to have been diminished by all this destruction, and it was this particular period that saw some of its greatest literary and artistic achievements. Internal evidence in the annals indicates that chroniclers at Clonmacnoise were keeping contemporary records of important events from at least the tenth century, and a number of surviving collections of annals were compiled and written originally here such as *The Annals of Tigernach*, called after an abbot of that name who died in 1088. The scriptorium must have produced many decorated gospel books and psalters over the centuries, but unfortunately none survives. However, some secular texts associated with the monastery have survived, in particular *Lebor na hUidre* or *The Book of the Dun Cow*. It contains mostly secular stories including the earliest extant version of Táin Bó Cuailgne. Its principal scribe was Mael Muire, a grandson of Conn na mBocht, who was slain by marauders in one of the churches at Clonmacnoise in 1106. The sculptured crosses and the bulk of the cross-slabs were also produced during this period after 800 AD, and much fine metalwork of which some examples survive.

Royal patronage is clearly in evidence at Clonmacnoise around 900, when the High King Flann was associated with the carving of the Cross of the Scriptures and the building of the stone church (the cathedral?). The cross still has a damaged inscription recording the event. From the eleventh century on, more detailed information on the site is recorded in the annals. For example, in 1026 the paved way from the Abbess's Yard to the Cairn of the Three Crosses was made by Abbot Breasal. Two further causeways, one from the cross of Bishop Etchen to Irdom Chiaráin, and the other from the Cairn of the Three Crosses to the Cross of Congal, were made by Mael-Chiaráin, son of Conn na mBocht, in 1070. The great stone church was covered with shingles in 1104. The round tower was completed in 1124, and a collection of treasures was stolen from the high altar in 1129. These were found with one of the foreigners of Limerick the following year, and returned. The thief was hanged by the king of Munster. In 1135 the top of the round tower was struck by lightning, while in 1149 the yew tree of St Ciarán suffered a similar fate and 113 sheep under it were killed.

CLONMACNOISE BECOMES A DIOCESE

The twelfth century witnessed a new reform movement in the Irish Church, involving both a shift in power from the old monasteries with their paruchiae, to newly set up dioceses ruled by bishops, and the introduction of religious orders from the continent such as Cistercians and Augustinians. In 1111 Clonmacnoise became the cathedral church of the western part of Meath, but the transition from monastery to diocesan centre appears to have been both slow and difficult. None of the new continental orders became established here, with the result that the establishment of the bishopric led to the gradual extinction of monastic life in the settlement. Plundering of the monastery continued during all of this period, and the Normans are recorded as plundering it on four occasions between 1178 and 1203, during one of which 105 houses were burned. In 1132 a Norman, Simon Rochfort, was made bishop of Clonard (Meath), and soon began extending his diocese westwards at the expense of Clonmacnoise so that, before long, the diocese consisted of little more than Delbna Ethra, the territory of the local ruling family, the Mac Coghlans.

A serious attempt to conquer the area was made by the Normans in 1214 when they defeated O Melaghlin, the overlord of the Mac Coghlans in battle, and first erected a castle at Clonmacnoise. It was apparently built on diocesan land, because, two years later, the king ordered the chief governor of Ireland to compensate the bishop for the land involved and 'for his fruit trees cut down, his cows, horses, oxen, and the household utensils taken away'. It was a royal castle, but very little documentation survives regarding it, the last mention of it being in 1233. The Norman family of Tuite claimed this entire area and built other castles in the barony. They were, however, driven out with the revival of Gaelic power towards the end of the thirteenth and into the fourteenth centuries, after which the Mac Coghlans controlled the area until the seventeenth century.

The Cathedral as seen from the top of the
round tower, with Temple Melaghlin and
Temple Dowling in the background

An early nineteenth-century engraving
showing the Pattern Green, now part of the
new graveyard, with the principal
monuments in the background. Based on an
original drawing by George Petrie.

14

The Decline of Clonmacnoise

A carving of a sheep's head on the remains of the fifteenth-century vaulting at the east end of the Cathedral

THE SETTLEMENT APPEARS TO HAVE DECLINED DRAMATICALLY FROM THE thirteenth century on. It was no longer one of the most important monasteries in Ireland, benefiting from the patronage of powerful kings, but the centre of one of the smallest and poorest dioceses in the country, in a small Gaelic lordship cut off politically from the main centres of wealth and trade. The poverty of the place is exemplified in a bardic poem about the cemetery, in which the poet complains of being sent away empty-handed by the clerics there:

> I give thanks to the king of heaven,
> to God I give thanks,
> for having come to the king of Tuam, with whom I am,
> from the paupers of Cluain Ciarán.

No doubt it continued as an important place of pilgrimage in the locality, but its national importance was largely in the past. It did not miss out entirely on the great building boom of the fifteenth century, for it was then that the beautiful north doorway and the vaulting at the east end were added to the cathedral.

As with many areas under Gaelic or Old English control, the Reformation had little or no affect on Clonmacnoise which remained in Catholic hands. This was presumably why the English garrison at Athlone plundered and devastated it in 1552, after which, in the words of the annalist, 'There was not left moreover, a bell, small or large, an image, or an altar, or a book, or a gem, or even glass in a window, from the wall of the church out, which was not carried off'. The Church of Ireland diocese of Clonmacnoise was united with Meath in 1569, a situation that has continued to the present day.

Clonmacnoise came to prominence again for a brief period in the middle of the seventeenth century. After the 1641 rebellion, the Catholic clergy gained control of much ecclesiastical property in the country, including Clonmacnoise, and a wall plaque in the cathedral records the repair of the building by the Catholic vicar general, Charles Coghlan, in 1647. In the following year the papal nuncio, Rinuccini, arrived at the site by boat, and met the bishop, Anthony Mac Geoghegan there. In December 1649, alarmed by the arrival of Cromwell in Ireland with a large army, the Catholic bishops assembled at Clonmacnoise and issued decrees encouraging all factions to unite against Cromwell. The Cromwellians overran the entire country, and Clonmacnoise again fell into ruin.

The earliest surviving detailed map of the site is that published in the second edition of James Ware's *De Hibernia et antiquitatibus eius disquisitiones* in 1658. This shows the graveyard already enclosed by a wall, and depicts and names ten churches, three of which have since been removed without trace. The map is a bird's eye view showing the buildings in three dimensions, but the architectural details are mostly fanciful, and the fact that they are shown with roofs should not be regarded as evidence that they were roofed at this time. The round tower has clearly been misrepresented by the engraver as a strange projection in the surrounding wall. The tower attached to Temple Finghin is shown, as are two crosses – the Cross of the Scriptures and another in the south-east sector of the graveyard where there is none today. The earliest detailed account we have of the churches at Clonmacnoise is that written by Anthony Dopping, Church of Ireland bishop of Meath in 1684. The cathedral was in ruin, as were all the eight other churches he listed, apart from Temple Ciarán where St Ciarán's Hand was kept, and what he called Temple Hurpan. In 1689, what we call Temple Dowling today, was rebuilt and roofed, as the plaque on it records. This was still in use as the Church of Ireland parish church in 1738, but by 1779 it had been abandoned in favour of the larger Temple Connor, which was again reconstructed in the early 19th century and is still in use.

In Harris's edition of the works of James Ware, first published in 1739, there is a plate showing a view and plan of the site and drawings of individual features and structures. These were drawn by Jonas Blaymires the previous year, and are a remarkable record of the monuments showing, for example, that the rafters of the roof of Temple Ciarán were still in place. It was not until the 19th century that the full importance of the site was appreciated, and antiquarians such as George Petrie began recording the cross slabs and their inscriptions. The chancel arch of the Nuns' Church, in a precarious state with only one order of the arch complete since before 1738, finally fell in the mid-19th century, and the Kilkenny and SE of Ireland Archaeological Society issued an appeal for funds to repair it. In 1866 the chancel arch and doorway of this church were rebuilt by the society, and repairs were also carried out to the main group of buildings. In 1877 the church ruins and other remains were taken into State Care by the Office of Public Works. In 1955 the Representative Body of the Church of Ireland presented the graveyard, containing the main group of buildings, to the

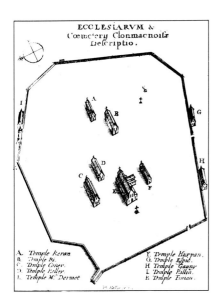

The earliest plan of the churches, published by Ware in 1658

State, and this now forms the core of the National Monument. A visitor centre, to the west of the graveyard, now houses the crosses and a selection of the cross-slabs to protect them from weather, theft and vandalism, while replicas of the crosses stand in the original locations.

Clonmacnoise continues to be a place of pilgrimage, and large crowds gather here each year for the Pattern (patron) day ceremonies in memory of St Ciarán. Pope John Paul II visited the site in 1979, during his visit to Ireland.

The Pattern Day at Clonmacnoise

An engraving of 1739 with a plan and views of the monuments based on originals by Blaymires

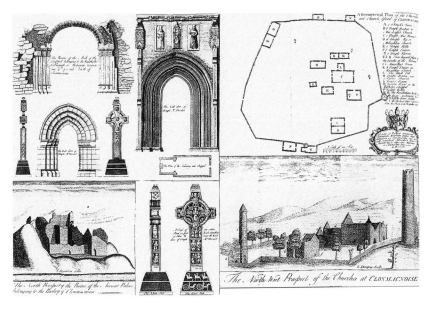

Map of Clonmacnoise

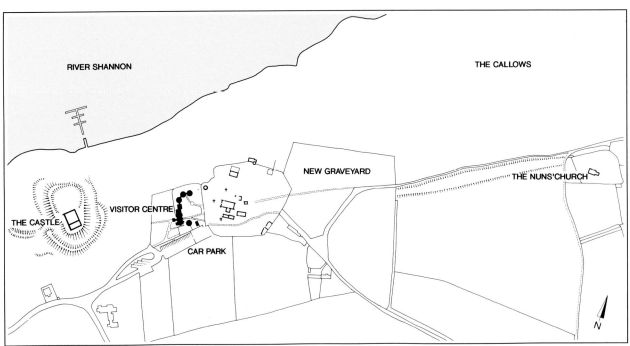

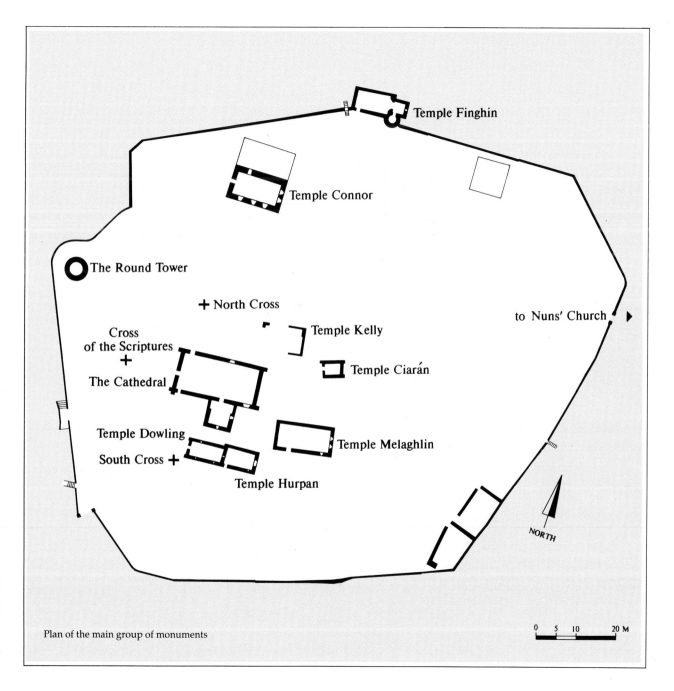

Temple Finghin

Temple Connor

The Round Tower

North Cross

Temple Kelly

Cross
of the Scriptures

Temple Ciarán

The Cathedral

to Nuns' Church

Temple Dowling

Temple Melaghlin

South Cross

Temple Hurpan

NORTH

Plan of the main group of monuments

0   5   10   20 M

Reconstruction showing Clonmacnoise at its peak

The Nature of the Settlement

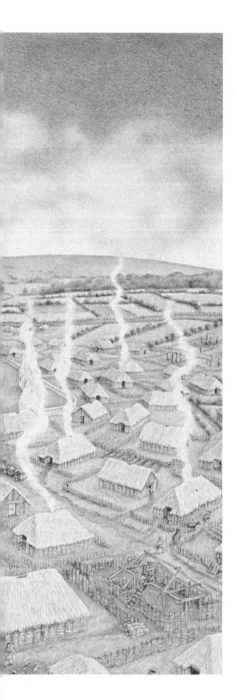

W HEN LOOKING AT CLONMACNOISE TODAY, IT IS IMPORTANT TO remember that, with the exception of the ogham stone, the surviving monuments do not go back to the time of St Ciarán himself or near it. The cross slabs date mainly from the period between the eight and eleventh centuries. The crosses belong to a narrower span between c800 and c900 AD, while the churches and other buildings, with later additions in some cases, belong to different periods and architectural styles. Some are possibly as early as the tenth century, while major features were added to the cathedral as late as the fifteenth century. The buildings of St Ciarán's original monastery would have been constructed of timber or post-and-wattle, and, from the start, an enclosing element. probably a bank and fosse, would have been an important feature of the site. Evidence for enclosures, often an inner and outer enclosure, has been found in the cases of other comparable early monasteries, but no trace of an enclosure has as yet been found at Clonmacnoise, and its discovery must await future archaeological excavations. Excavation work already carried out has shown that the settlement, as indicated by archaeological deposits in the ground, extended over a wide area from close to the modern school and the castle on the west side, to the far end of the new graveyard on the east side. The Nuns' Church, with its convent of nuns, probably had a separate enclosure detached from the main settlement.

It is also important to understand that early Irish monasteries were not laid out as a large unified group of buildings such as was the norm with religious orders on the Continent. The formal layout, with the church on one side of the cloister garth and the domestic and other buildings ranged around the other three sides, was only introduced to Ireland in the twelfth century with the Cistercians and Augustinians. Prior to that, the layout of the buildings does not seem to have followed a definite plan, and even after the churches came to be built mainly in stone, the other buildings continued to be built of perishable materials and, hence, do not survive. Also, instead of building a larger church as the settlement grew, the practice was to build more small churches, leading to the multiplicity of churches that we see on many of these sites today.

The Churches and Other Buildings

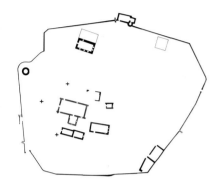

Tᴴᴇ ᴏʟᴅ ɢʀᴀᴠᴇʏᴀʀᴅ ᴄᴏɴᴛᴀɪɴs ᴍᴏsᴛ ᴏғ ᴛʜᴇ ᴍᴏɴᴜᴍᴇɴᴛs, ᴀɴᴅ ᴛʜɪs ᴀʀᴇᴀ was always the centre or focus of the settlement. The wall around the graveyard defines a polygonal area, and was already in existence in 1658. In the seventeenth- and early eighteenth-century plans of the site, the remains of eleven churches were shown within or attached to this boundary wall. Today the remains of only eight can be traced, and these are described below.

THE CATHEDRAL

This is by far the largest of the churches and is a simple rectangular structure measuring 18.8 x 8.7 metres internally. Noteworthy features are the antae (projecting sidewalls) visible at the east and west ends. These are a common feature of pre-Norman churches in Ireland. Also apparently original to the building are the putlock holes in the north and west walls. These held timbers which supported scaffolding during construction, and can be seen also in Temple Ciarán and in the Cathedral at Glendalough.

A close examination of the building reveals that the original south wall was two metres further south than at present, giving internal dimensions of 18.8 x 10.7 metres. The church was still its full size in the very early thirteenth century, when its original west doorway was replaced by an elaborate transitional style doorway of four orders, and the oldest part of the present sacristy was added on the south side. At a later stage, probably in the late thirteenth or early fourteenth century, the south wall was totally rebuilt where it now is, two metres in from its original line, and it was finished off with antae at each end for the sake of symmetry. The west door, however, ended up totally off-centre. The sacristy was extended up to the new south wall, its doorway having been rebuilt in the latter wall along with two new arched niches forming sedilia. The simple two-light window at the east end of the south wall is a later insertion of the fourteenth or early fifteenth century.

The later fifteenth century saw major additions being made to the

The elaborate fifteenth-century north doorway of the Cathedral

An internal view of the south wall of the
Cathedral showing the doorway to the
sacristy and evidence of different building
phases

A detail of the carving on the north
doorway

building in the form of the elaborate north doorway, a finely vaulted masonry canopy supported on pillars over the east end, with a room above it, and a second storey with fireplace and chimney added to the sacristy. The north doorway is beautifully carved in limestone in the perpendicular gothic style, with deep and complicated mouldings around the pointed opening. Above are carvings of St Dominic, St Patrick and St Francis, each identified by an inscription. A further inscription reads: 'DNS ODO DECANUS FIERI FECIT', indicating that a dean called Odo commissioned this work. This may be the same man as 'the dean O'Malone', who died in 1461. The vaulting at the east end is now mostly destroyed and some of what remains is baldly damaged, probably by fire.

The original building could be as early as 909 when, according to the *Chronicon Scotorum* (a collection of annals with close associations with Clonmacnoise), a stone church was built by King Flann and Abbot Colmán.

Two of the last high kings of Ireland, both also kings of Connacht, were buried here – Turlough O'Connor in 1156 and his son Rory O'Connor, who was buried on the north side of the altar here in 1198. The latter, who was the last high king of Ireland, abdicated in 1183 and spent his final years in retirement in the Augustinian abbey of Cong. In 1207 his remains were disinterred and deposited in a stone shrine, and this may well be the occasion when the transitional west doorway and sacristy were added to the building.

View of west door by Blaymires (1738). Most of the arch was removed early in the nineteenth century.

THE ROUND TOWER

The tower is situated in the north-west corner of the present graveyard and is finely built of well-shaped limestone blocks. It is 5.6 metres in diameter at the base, and tapers evenly towards the present top which is just over 19 metres high. As is usually the case with these towers, the doorway is well above ground level (in this case 3.3 metres) and is facing towards the main west door of the principal church on the site. In Irish sources, the word used for a round tower is cloigtheach (belfry), but the bells rung from the top storey would have been small hand bells.

The high doorways in these towers would have served as defensive features, and during attacks monks often sought refuge in round towers with their books and other valuables. There would have been wooden floors within the towers, with ladders connecting them. The top storey usually had four openings facing the cardinal points below a conical stone roof. *The Annals of the Four Masters* record that this round tower was completed in 1124 by Ua Maoleoin, successor of Ciarán. This would fit with

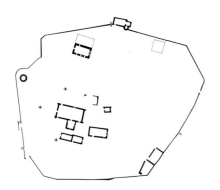

current thinking on the dating of these towers. In 1135 its top was struck off by lightning, which would help to explain why the present upper storey, with its eight openings, was added in later medieval times.

TEMPLE KELLY AND TEMPLE CIARÁN

Temple Ciarán with its projecting sidewalls or antae

An interior view of the east end of Temple Melaghlin with its fine pair of windows in the West of Ireland transitional style

Only fragmentary remains of the walls of Temple Kelly survive, close to the north-east corner of the cathedral. This church is possibly that erected by Conchobhar Ua Ceallaigh and the Uí Maine, in the place of the Dearthach (wooden oratory) in 1167. Between this church site and the cathedral there is a bullaun stone, set level with the surface of the ground. Such stones, with rounded depressions in them, sometimes holding water, are of uncertain use but are commonly found at early church sites.

The strangely contorted structure further east is Temple Ciarán, the smallest of the churches. Like the cathedral, this has antae and putlock holes, and is built largely of sandstone in a masonry style similar to the cathedral with which it is probably contemporary. The walls have shifted badly out of plumb, probably due to earlier and subsequent burial activity, and few features survive, the south wall and south half of the west wall being modern. The church measures 3.8 x 2.8 metres internally.

This is traditionally the location of St Ciarán's grave, the soil from which was formerly in great demand for its alleged curative and other beneficial properties. In 1684 this church was roofed and a relic, known as St Ciarán's Hand, was kept in it. The print of 1738 shows only the rafters of the roof in place.

TEMPLE MELAGHLIN

To the south of Temple Ciarán and south-east of the cathedral is Temple Melaghlin or Temple Ri, meaning the king's church. This is a simple rectangular church built very much in the Irish as opposed to Anglo-Norman tradition, with windows only in the east wall and the east end of the south wall.

The two tall round-headed windows in the east wall, with the continuous moulding all around them on the inside, belong to a transitional style of architecture peculiar to the west of Ireland and dating from the early years of the thirteenth century. The doorway in the south wall shows evidence of having been rebuilt. The corbels at the outer

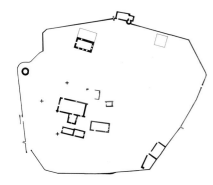

The Round Tower with its high-level
doorway, and the Cross of the Scriptures

Temple Dowling and the South Cross from
the north-west

The interior of Temple Dowling with its east
window and early steep gable incorporated
in the later gable of Temple Hurpan

corners would have served the same purpose as antae – to hold the barge boards of the roof – and are another Irish feature of the building. The Melaghlins, after whom the church is named, were the kings of Meath and overlords of the Mac Coghlans.

TEMPLE DOWLING AND TEMPLE HURPAN

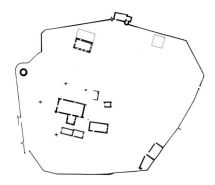

The original or eastern part of Temple Dowling is built of large facing stones in a style common among pre-Norman masonry churches in Ireland, and very different from the early masonry of the cathedral and Temple Ciarán. The steeply-pointed east gable with its round-headed window survives along with evidence that the building had antae. The church, originally 4.9 metres long by 3.45 metres wide, internally, was extended westwards by over 3 metres in 1689 by Edmund Dowling of Clondalare, as recorded on a plaque set up at the time over the pointed doorway. Interestingly, this 17th-century extension also has antae, in sympathy with the original.

An inscribed grave slab, partly visible in the interior of the north wall, appears to have been reused as a building stone in the original church. This was read as: [OR D] O DITHRAID (a prayer for Dithraid) by Petrie in the last century. The church takes its name from the man who rebuilt it in the seventeenth century, but its original name may have been Temple Hurpan, as Macalister suggests. The latter name is now applied to a strange, late church-like building added on to the east end of Temple Dowling. The west jamb of its doorway in the south wall is part of the antae of the older church.

TEMPLE CONNOR

This church appears to have been connected with the O'Connors of Connacht. It is a plain rectangular church, measuring 10.90 x 6.02 metres internally, and has been roofed and in use by the Church of Ireland since about the middle of the eighteenth century. The walls attached to it on the north enclose the burial place of the Malone family. The transitional arched west doorway of c1200, and a window at the east end of the south wall, are the only ancient openings to survive.

TEMPLE FINGHIN

This is the remains of a very interesting twelfth-century Romanesque church with an attached round tower built at the same time as the rest of the church at the junction of the nave and chancel on the south side. There may have been an earlier church on this same site, for there is an annalistic reference under the year 1013 that the great oak of Finghin's churchyard was overturned by a storm. The walls of the nave survive to only a few feet in height and only the basal stones of the Romanesque south doorway which was in three orders. The east wall of the nave with its Romanesque chancel arch in three orders is quite complete. The original carved sandstone of the arch has suffered damage in the past, possibly partly from fire, and the inner order was rebuilt in plain limestone in late medieval or early post medieval times. The chancel is finely built and quite complete, and a doorway at ground level here gives access to the round tower which was the belfry of the church. This has survived remarkably well to the tip of its conical stone roof. Part of the inner arch of a finely decorated Romanesque window is displayed on the west wall of the nave but may not belong at all to this church.

* * * * *

Detail of a grotesque animal's head biting a column of the chancel arch of Temple Finghin

OTHER STRUCTURES IN THE GRAVEYARD

In the south east corner of the graveyard are displayed the foundations of medieval residential buildings identified on the 1738 map as belonging to the dean and archdeacon. The same map shows three other churches which do not survive today, all forming part of the graveyard boundary. These were Temple Killin, just east of Temple Finghin, and Temple Gauny and Temple Espic, both against the south wall of the graveyard. Leading from close to Temple Ciarán eastwards and through the new graveyard is the line of an old roadway partly paved with large stones known as the Pilgrim's Way. Beyond the graveyard this has a tarred surface and gives access to the Nun's Church. This was one of the main approach roads to Clonmacnoise in earlier times. There is a bullaun stone deeply buried in the ground on the left verge of the road, not far beyond the new graveyard, while about midway along, on a narrow gravel ridge flanking the road on the right, is a small platform of stones which has been identified as the Cairn of the Three Crosses, mentioned in the annals.

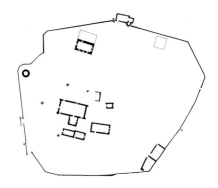

Temple Finghin with its Romanesque
chancel arch and attached round tower

The Nuns' Church with its fine Romanesque doorway and chancel arch

A detail of the chancel arch of the Nuns' Church showing an exhibitionist female figure at the top left

THE NUNS' CHURCH

This is situated in a small field adjoining the Pilgrim's Way, about one third of a mile east of the main site, and comprises the remains of a beautiful 12th-century Romanesque church with nave and chancel. The annals record that in 1167 this church was completed by Dearbhforgaill, a daughter of O'Melaghlin. The wife of Tighearnán O'Rourke, king of Breifne, she was abducted (apparently not unwillingly) by Dermot Mac Murrough, king of Leinster, during a raid in 1152. According to the *Annals of Clonmacnoise*, he 'kept her for a long space to satisfie his insatiable, carnall and adulterous lust'. She was returned to her husband the following year but he never forgave the insult, and when the opportunity arose in 1166, O'Rourke and his allies drove Mac Murrough out of his kingdom into exile. Mac Murrough enlisted the help of the Normans to regain his kingdom, and thus came about the Norman invasion in 1169. Dearbhforgaill was also a benefactor of the Cistercian abbey of Mellifont, to which she retired in 1186 and where she died in 1193, aged 85.

A human face on a chancel arch capital in the Nuns' Church

The Nuns' Church has a finely carved west doorway and chancel arch in the Irish Romanesque style. The decoration is largely abstract but includes some animal heads and an exhibitionist female figure on one of the voussoirs of the chancel arch. Only one order of this arch remained by 1738, and after this fell in the middle of the nineteenth century, the arch and doorway were reconstructed by the Kilkenny Archaeological Society, the missing sandstone voussoirs being replaced in limestone. A plaque over the doorway records this important work.

Considerable remains of the north wall of a second and earlier church here can be seen in the field fence to the south east. This was probably the stone church in the Cemetery of the Nuns, which, according to the annals, was burned in 1082.

THE CASTLE

This comprises a rectangular stone keep with a walled enclosure attached on the north or river side, and all contained within a massive D-shaped earthwork. The impressive ditch of this earthwork would probably have been partly water-filled originally, as still happens during high winter flood levels. The first castle built here in 1214 may have been a timber structure within this earthwork, which presumably was soon replaced by the present masonry structure. The rectangular keep had a forebuilding

The castle from the south

An aerial view of the castle with its
impressive earthworks

attached within the courtyard on the north side, which gave access to a high level main door into the keep. Slots for a small laterally-set drawbridge in front of the main door survive in the upper part of the wall of the forebuilding. One of the most notable and photogenic features of this castle is the south-west corner of the keep, which is undermined but has remained balanced in a manner that appears to defy gravity. It is usually stated that this castle was blown up with gunpowder in the sixteenth or seventeenth centuries, but without any supporting evidence. Another possibility is that it was undermined during the Gaelic resurgence around 1300 in this area, a theory that would find support in the complete lack of features later than the thirteenth century in this building, and the lack of later references to the castle.

ST CIARÁN'S WELL

This well, now often dry, is situated about a quarter of a mile from the main site on the river side of the Shannonbridge road on private land. There is an early cross-slab here along with a limestone cross and bust of St Ciarán in the folk art tradition of about two hundred years ago.

St Ciarán's Well

The Crosses and Slabs

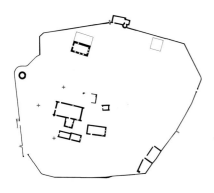

THERE WERE FOUR CROSSES MARKED ON THE 1738 PLAN, THREE OF WHICH were in the same positions until 1992-93, when they were removed into the visitor centre and replaced by replicas. These are The Cross of the Scriptures in front of the Cathedral, the South Cross at the south-west corner of Temple Dowling and the North Cross (shaft only) to the north of the Cathedral. The fourth cross was marked to the south-east of Temple Melaghlin and nothing certain is known about it. Three other cross fragments are known from the site, one of which is now in the National Museum.

THE CROSS OF THE SCRIPTURES

This is one of Ireland's finest surviving high crosses, named on the assumption that it is the cross of that name referred to in the annals under the year 1060. The inscriptions on the east and west faces of the base of the shaft are badly damaged, but have been convincingly reconstructed to read continuously, starting on the west side:

> 'OR DO RIG FLAIND MAC MAELSECHNAILL OROIT DO RIG HERENN OR DO COLMAN DORRO ... IN CROSSA AR ... RIG FLAIND'.
> (A prayer for King Flann, son of Maelsechnaill, a prayer for the king of Ireland. A prayer for Colmán who made this cross for King Flann).

Flann Sinna mac Maelsechnaill was King of Meath and High King of Ireland from 879 to 916. The Colmán mentioned could either have been the sculptor of the cross or the abbot of that name who ruled Clonmacnoise from c904 to 926. It is tempting to see the cross being carved at the same time as the Cathedral was built, in 909, probably in thanksgiving for Flann's resounding victory over the king of Munster at Belach Mugna the previous year.

The shaft and head of the cross are carved from one piece of sandstone, and this is slotted into the sandstone base which takes the form of a truncated pyramid. A ring surrounds the junction of the arms and shaft, as

The Cross of the Scriptures – a view of the south side

is usually the case with Irish high crosses, but in this case the arms have a unique upward tilt which adds lightness and vibrancy to the form.

All sides of the cross and base are covered with decoration, mostly depictions of human figures in panels, either singly or in groups. All of these figured panels would have had a definite meaning for the sculptor's contemporaries, but now the meaning of many of them, especially on this cross, is elusive. Some are clearly recognisable as biblical scenes and have parallels on other crosses, but others are open to various interpretations whether biblical, historical or allegorical.

On the west face, the centre of the crosshead within the ring has a crucifixion with the sponge and lance bearers at each side of Christ. The three panels on the shaft, starting from the bottom, show Christ in the tomb just prior to the resurrection; a scene with three figures, possibly the flagellation of Christ; and lastly, the soldiers casting lots for Christ's clothes. At the centre of the crosshead on the east face is the figure of Christ in judgement, with the blessed on one side and the damned on the other. A puzzling scene is that above the inscription at the base of the shaft showing two figures, in contrasting attire, grasping a pole. It is most often interpreted as King Diarmaid helping St Ciarán to build his first church, but is more likely to be Aaron, Moses and the brazen serpent. Above this is a scene with two figures of uncertain significance; below a scene with Christ handing Peter a key and Paul a book.

There are further worn scenes on the base, in particular two horse-drawn chariots on the east face below three men on horses. On the south side of the base are two scenes: the kiss of Judas above a hunting scene.

The Cross of the Scriptures. Panel showing King Diarmaid and St Ciarán or, more likely, Aaron, Moses and the brazen serpent.

opposite, left
The Cross of the Scriptures from the west

opposite, right
The Cross of the Scriptures from the east

THE SOUTH CROSS

Chronologically, this is an earlier type of high cross with mainly abstract ornament. There is only one figured scene and that is on the west face of the shaft just below the crosshead; it is a depiction of the crucifixion. This cross is closely akin to the Ahenny group of crosses and all have features apparently derived from metal-encased wooden crosses. While some scholars would argue for a date around or even before 800 for this cross, others would favour a date further into the ninth century, and a recent reading of some of the letters of the very badly damaged inscription at the base of the west face of the shaft suggests that it may have been commissioned by the high king Maelsechnaill Mac Maelruanaid, the father of Flann, who is named on the Cross of the Scriptures. He was High King from 846 to 862.

The South Cross from the west

The shaft and crosshead are again formed from one piece of sandstone slotting into a large base stone in the form of a truncated pyramid. The house-shaped cap in this case is a separate piece of stone. Virtually the entire surface is covered with ornament in panels with various types of interlace, fret and spiral patterns abounding. The head is ornamented with five large hemispherical bosses on each face, at the points where, on a wooden or metalwork cross, functional rivets would have held it together. The base is very worn but has both abstract and representational ornament, including figures on horses.

THE NORTH CROSS

Only the shaft of this cross survives with the remains of a tenon at the top, over which the head, with a corresponding mortise in its underside, would have fitted. The stone of the shaft has veins of harder material running through it, and these stand out where the remainder has eroded slightly. Only three sides of the shaft are decorated; the fourth, the east side, is totally blank. The reason for this is unknown but it may originally have stood against a building. The repertoire of ornament includes interlaced human figures, animals and panels with interlacing designs. This, along with two related fragments from the site and the Banagher shaft and the Bealin cross, are the products of one workshop and have been dated to around 800. The animals have parallels on carved slabs in Scotland, while other aspects of the decoration, including the human figures, have parallels in the Book of Kells.

Excavation around the north cross in 1990 revealed that the shaft is set in a large round sandstone base which had been totally buried beneath the surface in modern times. This was originally a millstone. It appears to have been shaped to take a box-like superstructure rising 0.3 metres above the present top of the base, to the level of the first panel. Parallels for this feature are found at Iona in Scotland.

OTHER SHAFT FRAGMENTS

The largest of these is a shaft, part of which was apparently in Temple Dowling in 1909. It is decorated on one face only with lions and a mounted horseman, in a style very similar to the north cross. There is a shaft fragment from the site with abstract ornament only on three sides in the

The south side of the North Cross with (from top) a lion, an S-shaped spiral motif and a human figure with intertwined limbs.

The base of the North Cross as uncovered by excavation

A shaft with lions and a mounted horseman

A cross fragment with confronted lions

National Museum of Ireland

Another cross fragment comprises the upper part of the shaft of a cross close to its junction with the arms. It had hollows at the angles but no ring, and on one face is a remarkable design of two confronted lions with jaws and legs intertwining. The other three sides have interlace designs. There is disagreement as to the dating of this fragment, with some opting for a date around 800 while others hold that the lions are carved in Hiberno-Romanesque style and date from the twelfth century.

THE OGHAM STONE

This was found during the digging of a grave in the new cemetery in May 1990. It is a large rectangular piece of sandstone with a short damaged ogham inscription on one edge. The ogham alphabet is based on the Latin alphabet and first appears in Ireland around the 4th century AD. The language used is an early form of Irish, and the letters are formed of strokes (1 to 5) variously arranged on the corner of a stone. The inscription in this case is damaged, but the letters NADAV... can be made out. Ogham stones are found mainly in south Munster, and this example is the first from Co Offaly. It may date from as early as the fifth or sixth century and is probably the oldest monument on the site. The stone was subsequently used for sharpening iron implements .

THE GRAVESLABS

This is the largest and most remarkable collection of pre Norman graveslabs in Britain or Ireland. Over 600 slabs or fragments of slabs are known. They range in date from about 700 up until the twelfth century, and include fine examples of all the major types of early graveslabs known from Ireland. Many are exceptionally well executed, and clearly there was a school of craftsmen carving graveslabs at Clonmacnoise over a number of centuries. They are virtually all of sandstone, possibly got from Bloomhill a few miles to the north-east. Generally the stone is not shaped or dressed but is carved on a natural and sometimes partly uneven face. Some of the individuals commemorated in the inscriptions can be identified in the annals, thus giving dates for some of the graveslabs. The inscriptions are in Irish in what is known as the half uncial script, and generally follow the formula 'OROIT DO X' (A prayer for X), usually contracted to 'OR DO X'.

The earliest slabs, some dating possibly from as early as the 7th century, have either small outline crosses or just a small cross at the start of the inscription known as an initial cross. A very interesting example of this group has the name Colmán after an initial cross, with the word *bocht* (poor) following it, written in the ogham script on a line inscribed on the face of the stone. This is not an ogham stone in the proper sense of the word but an example of scholastic ogham as is found also in manuscripts.

Crosses in square or rectangular frames are common from the site and date mainly from the eighth and ninth centuries. Another large group has ringed crosses and these date mainly from the ninth century. In the tenth and eleventh centuries, crosses with expanded terminals became the norm, and some of the finest slabs are of this type. Among these is the beautiful slab of Tuathal Saer (Tuathal the craftsman), which, unusually, is both dressed and shaped. Another slab has an evocative addition to the usual formula; it reads: 'OR DO FE[ID]ILMID' (a prayer for Feidilmid), with the following addition in Latin: 'QUI OCCISUS [EST] SINA CA [USA] ' (who was killed without cause). Although the slabs commemorating Kings Turlough and Rory O'Connor do not apparently survive, there is a drawing of a cross with expanded terminals in the margin of the manuscript of the *Annals of Tigernach*, at the point where Turlough's death is chronicled with a note describing it as his graveslab.

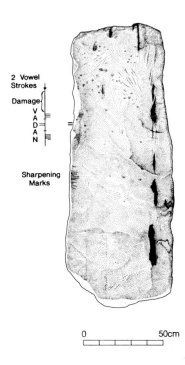

2 Vowel
Strokes

Damage

V
A
D
A
N

Sharpening
Marks

0   50cm

The ogham stone found in the new graveyard in 1990

The 'FEIDILMID' slab

A range of graveslabs (not to scale)

1 – A linear latin cross with triangular terminals and 'OR DO FINNACHTU'
2 – A cross of arcs in a circle with 'OR DO MUIRETHACH'
3 – An interlaced Greek cross with 'OR DO DANÉIL'
4 – A ringed cross with 'OR AR MAELQUIARÁIN'
5 – The slab of 'COLMAN BOCHT' which is preceded by a small initial cross. The word 'BOCHT' is in ogham writing.
6 – A finely shaped and dressed slab with a cross with expanded terminals and 'OR DO THUATHAL SAER'
7 – A cross with expanded terminals and no inscription
8 – A ringed cross in a square frame with a fretwork border. The inscription is damaged.
9 – A ringed cross with 'DUBINSE'

4

5

7

8

9

Artefacts associated with Clonmacnoise

ORNATE METALWORK

A number of finely decorated metalwork objects are said to have been found on or near the site and these include an openwork bronze plaque with a depiction of the crucifixion, a fragment of a crozier, a silver brooch and a hemispherical boss of gilt bronze. There is also the beautifully ornamented metal crozier, known as the Crozier of the Abbots of Clonmacnoise, which is traditionally associated with the site and dates originally from the late eleventh century.

The finely decorated metalwork shrine of the *Stowe Missal* has an inscription on it which states that Donnchadh Ua Taccain of the community of Cluain (Clonmacnoise) made it. Recent work on the inscription indicates that the manufacture of the shrine can be dated to between 1026 and 1033. The missal and its shrine were associated with the monastery of Lorrha in North Tipperary. Most of these objects are in the National Museum of Ireland in Dublin.

ARCHAEOLOGICAL EXCAVATION

A number of excavations have been carried out at the site. In 1979, when a hole was being dug for a new goal post in the playing field beside the National School, a hoard of silver coins was found. The find spot was subsequently excavated by Raghnall O'Floinn of the National Museum, who found that this area was part of the settlement when this hoard of Hiberno-Norse coins was hidden in the late eleventh century.

In 1985 and 1989-90, part of the Steeple Garden was excavated prior to the building of the new visitor centre. Evidence for iron smelting, bronze working, habitation, cultivation and a kiln were found. The activity here continued into the thirteenth century.

Rescue excavations have also been undertaken in the north-west corner of the new graveyard, in advance of its use for burial. The ogham stone was

A bronze and enamel escutcheon with an animal's head, from archaeological excavations in the new graveyard

left
The Crozier of the Abbots of Clonmacnoise

right
The shrine of the *Stowe Missal*

A bone trial or motif piece. Craftsmen would have learned their trade on such pieces of bone. Found during archaeological excavations prior to the building of the visitor centre.

The Office of Public Works

Written by   Conleth Manning

Design   John O'Regan
        (© Gandon Books, 1994)
Production   Nicola Dearey, Gandon Irish
        Art Books (Cork)

Photographs
Con Brogan and John Scarry,
    The Office of Public Works
National Museum (11, 47a, 47b)
The National Library (7, 8, 14)
Royal Irish Academy (10)
Con Manning (14b)

Surveying and Draughting
Fiachra Keyes, Caitríona Quinn and Gerald
    Woods
The Map of Clonmacnoise is based on the
    Ordnance Survey by permission of the
    Government. Permit no.5876.

Reconstruction illustration
Phelim Manning and Aislinn Adams

Acknowledgements
The author and The Office of Public Works
would like to thank the following for their
assistance with this publication: Heather
King, Marsh's Library, de Búrca Rare Books.

found in this area, and the subsequent excavations by Heather King have uncovered corn-drying kilns, traces of houses, a boat slip and an interesting array of finds.

SOURCES

There is no single up-to-date, reliable source on the history and antiquities of Clonmacnoise, nor is there room here to list all of the sources consulted during the compilation of this booklet. However, a few are worth mentioning: RAS Macalister's books on the slabs, *The Memorial Slabs of Clonmacnoise* (1909) and *Corpus Inscriptionum Insularum Celticarum*, vol.II (1949), have not been surpassed, though many slabs have been found since they were published. P Harbison's *The High Crosses of Ireland*, Bonn, 1992, is essential reading on the crosses. The history of Clonmacnoise is poorly served, with only Rev J Ryan's *Clonmacnois: A Historical Summary*, Dublin, 1973. For the general background, M and L de Paor's *Early Christian Ireland*, London, 1958; N Edwards' *The Archaeology of Early Medieval Ireland*, London, 1990; and K Hughes and A Hamlin's *The Modern Traveller to the Early Irish Church*, London, 1977, are useful, and all have bibliographies for further reading. For information on the natural history of the area, see M Tubridy, ed., *The Heritage of Clonmacnoise*, Dublin and Tullamore, 1987.

© 1994 Government of Ireland

Government Publications Sale Office
    Sun Alliance House, Molesworth Street
    Dublin 2

ISBN 0-7076-0388-9

Printed by Betaprint, Dublin

DUBLIN:
PUBLISHED BY THE STATIONERY OFFICE.

To be purchased through any Bookseller, or directly from the
GOVERNMENT PUBLICATIONS SALE OFFICE,
SUN ALLIANCE HOUSE, MOLESWORTH STREET, DUBLIN 2.

Price: £2.50